Australian Wildlife *i*

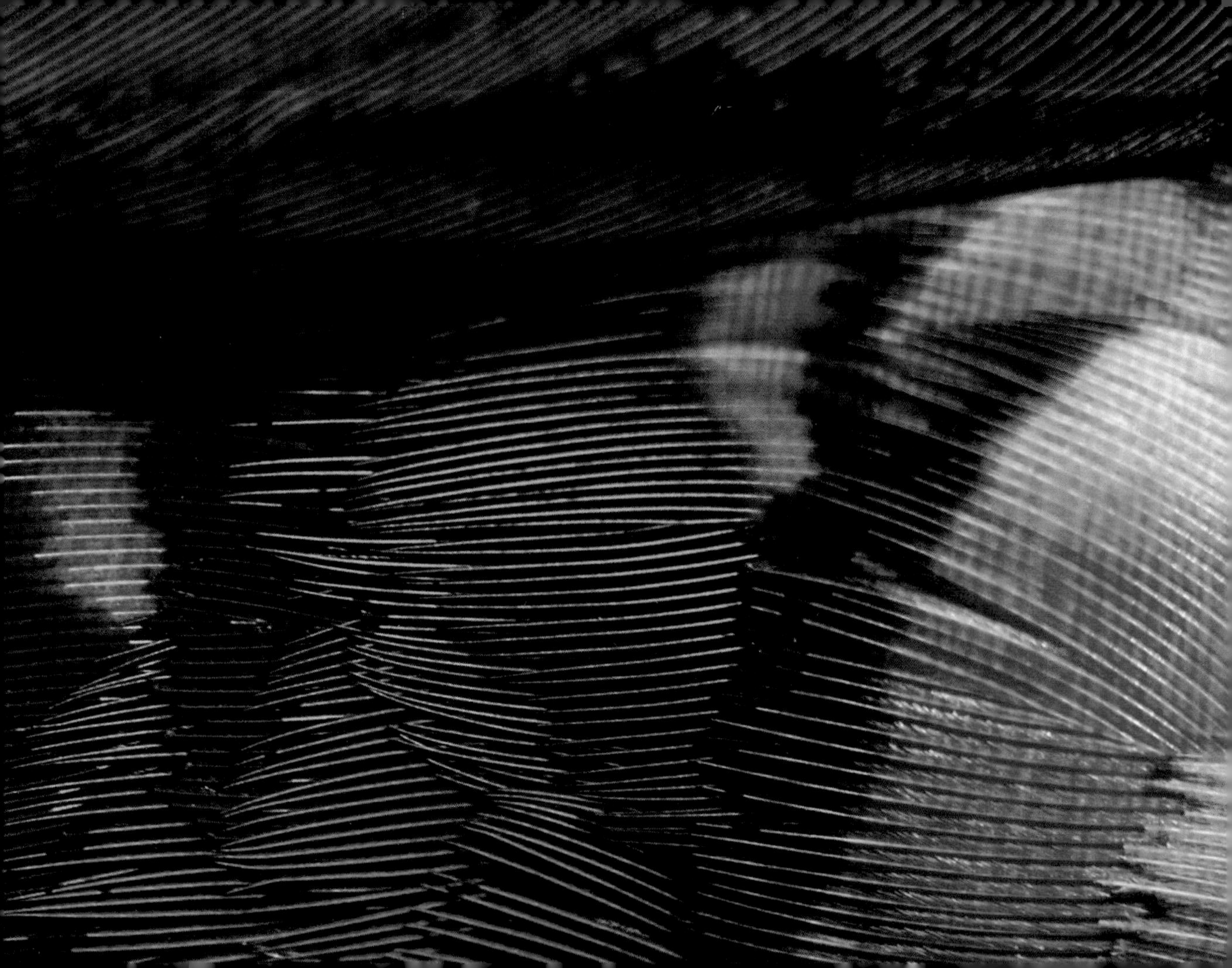

Australian
Wildlife
in pictures

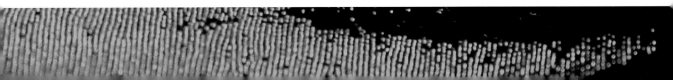

Introducing Australian Wildlife

Due to its long-term geographical isolation Australia has developed many unique forms of wildlife. This remarkable diversity has also been brought about by the fact that the country hosts such a wide variety of habitats, ranging from deserts through to alpine areas and encompassing tropical and temperate rainforests, woodlands, heathlands and ephemeral wetlands, plus of course marine environments which include kelp forests and the world's largest barrier reef system. As you will see from the pages of the book, it is a recipe that delivers natural wonders in abundance.

Australia's 'signature' species are known across the world, and animals such as koala, platypus, kangaroos, lyrebirds, cockatoos, taipans, death adders, dragons and crocodiles all feature here alongside less well-known wonders such as bilby, pardalotes, rainbow-skinks, snake-lizards, cowfish and much more. The flora is no less astounding and includes remarkable arid specialists in the desert areas, lush rainforest trees, mind-blowing orchids and a 'living fossil' in the shape of the Wollemi Pine, which was discovered alive and well not so far from Sydney in the 1990s despite having previously been known only from fossil records from circa 200 million years ago.

Australian Wildlife in Pictures provides an attractive introduction to this wide-ranging and spectacular subject. It includes illustrations of a cross-section of all key families of animals and plants. The names and classifications of these generally follow those used in Reed New Holland's excellent and comprehensive series of field guides, and in its other books on these subjects, and if you want to know more about any of the families covered then obtaining copies of these is definitely a good idea. Some of the key titles are listed on pages 250 and 251 of this book.

In the meantime we hope that you enjoy this book and its amazing images, and that it contributes towards inspiring further interest in Australia's stunning and unique natural history.

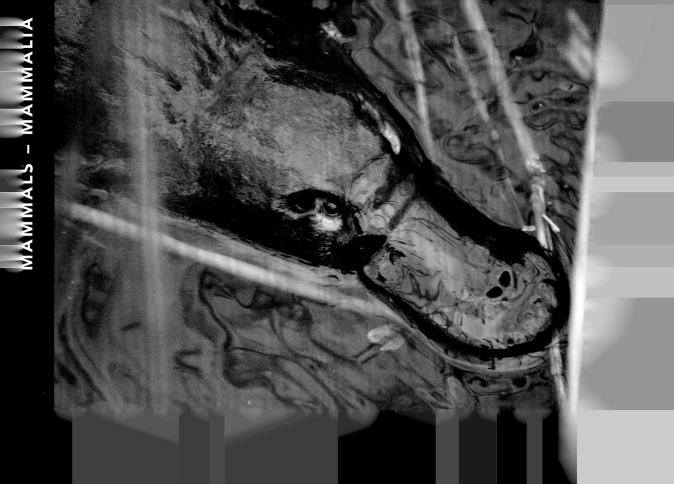

Short-beaked Echidna *Tachyglossus aculeatus*
AUSTRALIA-WIDE

Tasmanian Devil *Sarcophilus harrisii*
TASMANIA

Spotted-tailed Quoll *Dasyurus maculatus*
EASTERN AUSTRALIA

Subtropical Antechinus *Antechinus subtropicus*
SOUTH-EAST QUEENSLAND

Fat-tailed Dunnart *Sminthopsis crassicaudata*

Numbat *Myrmecobius fasciatus*
WESTERN AUSTRALIA

Southern Brown Bandicoot *Isoodon obesulus*
SOUTHERN AUSTRALIA

Bilby *Macrotis lagotis*
PATCHY DISTRIBUTION IN INLAND AUSTRALIA

Koala *Phascolarctos cinereus*
QUEENSLAND TO SOUTH AUSTRALIA

Common Wombat   *Vombatus ursinus*
NEW SOUTH WALES TO SOUTH AUSTRALIA AND TASMANIA

Eastern Pygmy Possum *Cercartetus nanus*
SOUTH-EAST AUSTRALIA

Striped Possum   *Dactylopsila trivirgata*

Sugar Glider *Petaurus breviceps*

NORTH AND EAST AUSTRALIA

Common Brushtail Possum *Trichosurus vulpecula*

AUSTRALIA-WIDE

Green Ringtail Possum *Pseudochirops archeri*

Woylie *Bettongia penicillata*

SOUTHERN AUSTRALIA

Long-nosed Potoroo *Potorous tridactylus*
EASTERN AUSTRALIA

Lumholtz's Tree-Kangaroo *Dendrolagus lumholtzi*

Eastern Grey Kangaroo *Macropus giganteus*
EASTERN AUSTRALIA

Bridled Nailtail Wallaby *Onychogalea fraenata*

Dugong *Dugong dugon*
COASTS IN NORTHERN HALF OF AUSTRALIA

Australian Sea Lion   *Neophoca cinerea*

SOUTHERN COASTS

Southern Right Whale *Eubalaena australis*
COASTS IN SOUTHERN HALF OF AUSTRALIA

Humpback Whale *Megaptera novaeangliae*
OCEANS AROUND AUSTRALIA

Southern Cassowary *Casuarius casuarius*
NORTH QUEENSLAND

Emu *Dromaius novaehollandiae*

AUSTRALIA-WIDE

Magpie Goose *Anseranas semipalmata*
NORTHERN AND EASTERN AUSTRALIA

Black Swan *Cygnus atratus*
AUSTRALIA-WIDE

Chestnut Teal *Anas castanea*
EASTERN AUSTRALIA AND WEST COAST

Musk Duck *Biziura lobata*
SOUTHERN AUSTRALIA

Australasian Grebe   *Tachybaptus novaehollandiae*

Diamond Dove *Geopelia cuneata*
AUSTRALIA-WIDE

Australian Bustard *Ardeotis australis*
AUSTRALIA-WIDE EXCEPT SOUTH-EAST

Channel-billed Cuckoo *Scythrops novaehollandiae*
NORTHERN AND EASTERN AUSTRALIA

Tawny Frogmouth *Podargus strigoides*
AUSTRALIA-WIDE

Australian Owlet-nightjar *Aegotheles cristatus*
AUSTRALIA-WIDE

Australian Crake *Porzana fluminea*

PATCHY DISTRIBUTION ACROSS AUSTRALIA

Brolga *Antigone rubicunda*
NORTHERN AND EASTERN AUSTRALIA

Pied Stilt · *Himantopus leucocephalus*
AUSTRALIA-WIDE

Masked Lapwing *Vanellus miles*
AUSTRALIA-WIDE

Inland Dotterel *Charadrius australis*
EASTERN AUSTRALIA

Eastern Curlew *Numenius madagascariensis*

AUSTRALIAN COASTS

Silver Gull *Chroicocephalus novaehollandiae*
AUSTRALIA-WIDE

Little Penguin *Eudyptula minor*
SOUTHERN COASTS

Wandering Albatross   *Diomedea exulans*
SEAS AROUND SOUTHERN AUSTRALIA

Wedge-tailed Shearwater *Ardenna pacifica*
EAST AND WEST COASTS

Pied Cormorant *Phalacrocorax varius*

White-faced Heron *Egretta novaehollandiae*
AUSTRALIA-WIDE

Yellow-billed Spoonbill *Platalea flavipes*
AUSTRALIA-WIDE

Powerful Owl *Ninox strenua*

SOUTH-EAST AUSTRALIA

Laughing Kookaburra *Dacelo novaeguineae*
EASTERN AND SOUTH-WEST AUSTRALIA

Sulphur-crested Cockatoo *Cacatua galerita*
NORTH, EAST AND SOUTH-WEST AUSTRALIA

Australian King-Parrot *Alisterus scapularis*
EASTERN AUSTRALIA

Rainbow Lorikeet *Tricholglossus haemotodus*

EAST COAST AND SOUTH-WEST AUSTRALIA

Budgerigar *Melopsittacus undulatus*
AUSTRALIAN INTERIOR

Regent Bowerbird *Sericulus chrysocephalus*

Superb Fairy-wren *Malurus cyaneus*

SOUTH-EAST AUSTRALIA

Varied Sittella *Daphoenositta chrysoptera*
AUSTRALIA-WIDE

Golden Whistler *Pachycephala pectoralis*
SOUTHERN AND EASTERN AUSTRALIA

Australasian Figbird *Sphecotheres vieilloti*
NORTHERN AND EASTERN AUSTRALIA

White-browed Woodswallow *Artamus superciliosus*
AUSTRALIA-WIDE

Australian Magpie *Gymnorhina tibicen*
AUSTRALIA-WIDE

Willie-wagtail *Rhipidura leucophrys*
AUSTRALIA-WIDE EXCEPT TASMANIA

Apostlebird *Struthidea cinerea*
EASTERN AND NORTHERN AUSTRALIA

Rose Robin *Petroica rosea*

SOUTH-EAST AUSTRALIA

Welcome Swallow *Hirundo neoxena*
AUSTRALIA-WIDE

Bassian Thrush *Zoothera lunulata*

EASTERN AND SOUTH-EAST AUSTRALIA

Olive-backed Sunbird   *Cinnyris jugularis*
NORTH-EAST AUSTRALIA

Beautiful Firetail *Stagonopleura bella*
SOUTH-EAST AUSTRALIA

REPTILES – REPTILIA

Saltwater Crocodile *Crocodylus porosus*
NORTHERN AUSTRALIA

Freshwater Crocodile   *Crocodylus johnstoni*
NORTHERN AUSTRALIA

Hawksbill Turtle *Eretmochelys imbricata*

WATERS AROUND AUSTRALIA EXCEPT SOUTH COAST

Northern Long-necked Turtle *Chelodina oblonga*
NORTHERN QUEENSLAND AND NORTHERN TERRITORY

Georges' Turtle *Wollumbinia georgesi*
BELLINGER RIVER, NEW SOUTH WALES

Smooth Knob-tailed Gecko *Nephrurus levis*
INTERIOR AUSTRALIA AND WEST COAST

Northern Leaf-tailed Gecko *Saltuarius cornutus*
NEAR COOKTOWN, QUEENSLAND

Eastern Stone Gecko *Diplodactylus vittatus*
EASTERN AUSTRALIA

Burton's Snake-Lizard *Lialis burtonis*
AUSTRALIA-WIDE

Closed-litter Rainbow Skink *Carlia longipes*
QUEENSLAND

Eastern Water Skink *Eulamprus quoyii*

Copper-tailed Skink *Ctenotus taeniolatus*

EASTERN AUSTRALIA

Jacky Lizard *Amphibolurus muricatus*

EASTERN AUSTRALIA

Frillneck *Chlamydosaurus kingii*
NORTHERN AUSTRALIA

Sand Monitor *Varanus gouldii*
AUSTRALIA-WIDE

Woma *Aspidites ramsayi*

INLAND AUSTRALIA

Olive Python *Liasis olivaceus*
NORTHERN AUSTRALIA

Top End Carpet Python *Morelia spilota variegata*
NORTHERN AUSTRALIA

Green Tree Python *Morelia viridis*
QUEENSLAND

Brown Tree Snake *Boiga irregularis*
NORTHERN AND EASTERN AUSTRALIA

Common Death Adder *Acanthopis antarcticus*

SOUTHERN AND EASTERN AUSTRALIA

Highlands Copperhead   *Austrelaps ramsayi*
SOUTH-EAST AUSTRALIA

Tiger Snake *Notechis scutatus*
SOUTHERN AUSTRALIA

Inland Taipan *Oxyuranus microlepidotus*
INLAND QUEENSLAND AND SOUTH AUSTRALIA

Common Bandy Bandy   *Vermicella annulata*

Yellow-bellied Sea Snake *Pelamis platura*
WATERS AROUND AUSTRALIA EXCEPT SOUTH COAST

Green-eyed Tree Frog *Litoria serrata*
QUEENSLAND

Orange-thighed Frog *Litoria xanthomera*
QUEENSLAND

Magnificent Tree Frog *Litoria splendida*
KIMBERLEY REGION

Waterfall Frog *Litoria nannotis*
QUEENSLAND

Spotted Marsh Frog *Limnodynastes tasmaniensis*
EASTERN AUSTRALIA

Northern Banjo Frog *Limnodynastes terraereginae*

EASTERN AUSTRALIA

Sudell's Frog *Neobatrachus sudelli*

SOUTHERN HALF OF AUSTRALIA

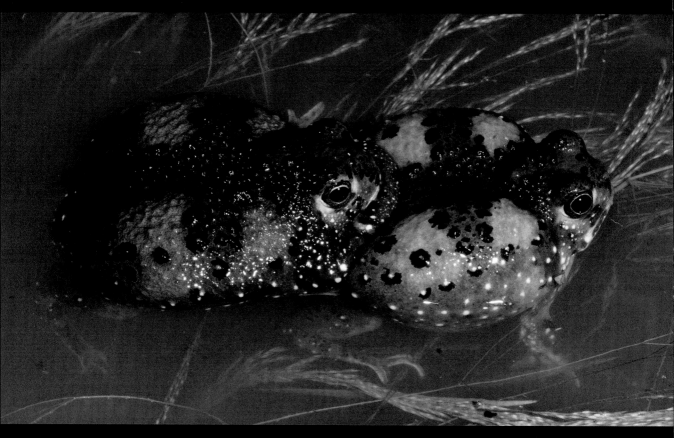

Crucifix Frog *Notaden bennetti*
EASTERN AUSTRALIA

Spotted Wobbegong *Orectolobus maculatus*
SEAS OFF SOUTH AND EAST AUSTRALIA

Whale Shark *Rhincodon typus*
SEAS OFF NORTHERN AUSTRALIA

Blue-spotted Fantail Ray *Taeniura lymna*

Ribbon Eel *Rhinomuraena quaesita*

SEAS OFF NORTH-EAST AUSTRALIA

Ornate Ghostpipefish *Solenostomus paradoxus*
NORTH AND CENTRAL COASTS

Weedy Seadragon *Phyllopteryx taeniolatus*
SOUTH COAST

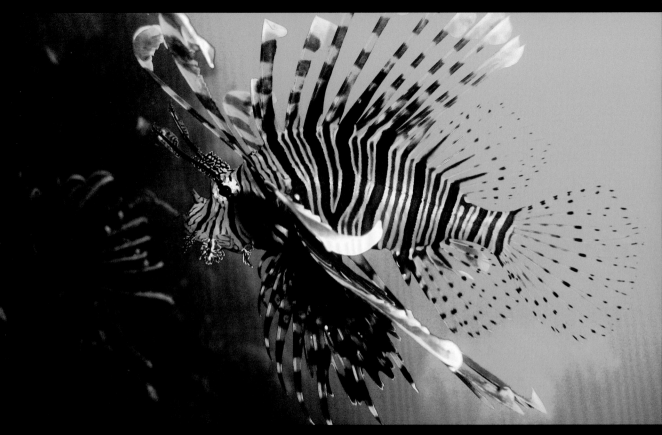

Common Lionfish *Pterois volitans*

SEAS OFF AUSTRALIA EXCEPT SOUTH COAST

Beaked Coralfish   *Chelmon rostratus*

NORTH AND EAST COASTS

Eastern Blue Groper *Achoerodus viridis*

Mandarinfish *Synchiropus splendidus*
QUEENSLAND COAST

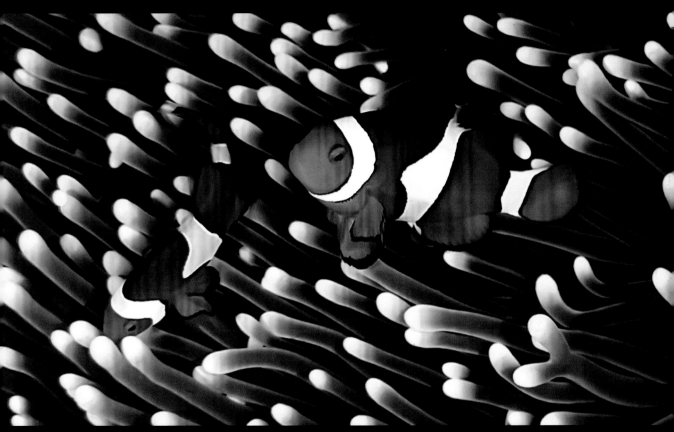

Eastern Clown Anemonefish *Amphiprion percula*
EAST COAST OF QUEENSLAND

Blue Tang *Paracanthurus hepatus*

EAST COAST

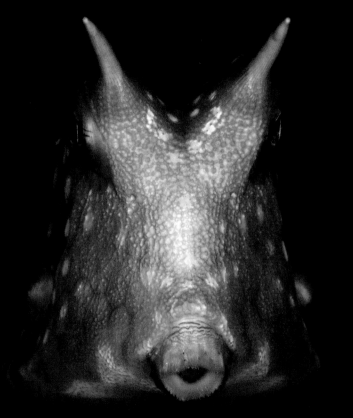

Longhorn Cowfish *Lactoria cornuta*
SEAS OFF AUSTRALIA EXCEPT SOUTH COAST

Australian Grayling *Prototroctes maraena*
RIVERS IN SOUTH-EAST AUSTRALIA

Southern Purple-spotted Gudgeon *Mogurnda adspersa*

RIVERS IN SOUTH-EAST AUSTRALIA

Australian Red-claw Crayfish *Cherax quadricarinatus*
NORTHERN AUSTRALIA

MOLLUSCS – MOLLUSCA

Cone shell species *Conus* sp.
AUSTRALIAN COASTS

Red-lined Bubble Snail *Bullina lineata*

AUSTRALIAN COASTS

Nudibranch species *Mexichromis* sp.

WATERS AROUND AUSTRALIA

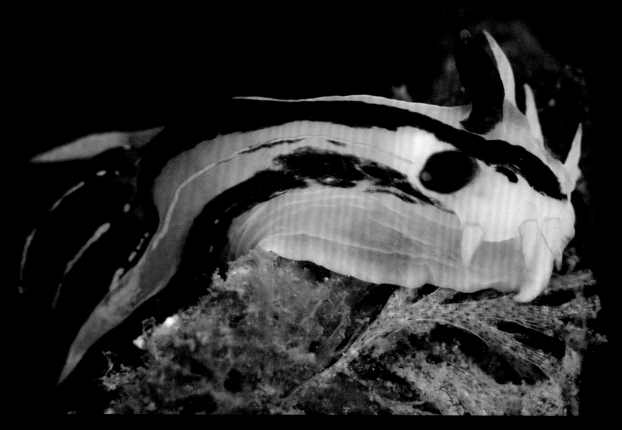

Crowned Nudibranch *Polycera capensis*
WATERS AROUND AUSTRALIA

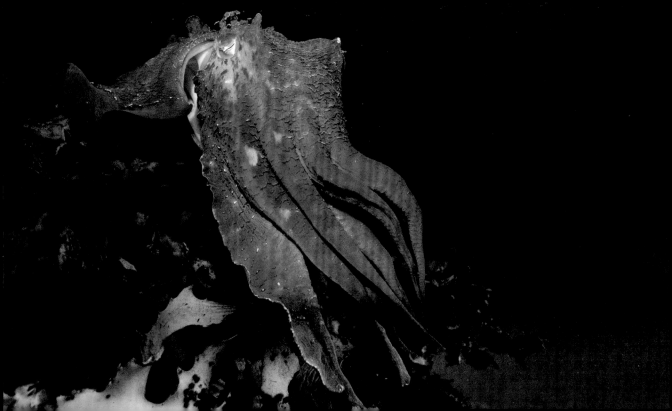

Australian Sea Apple *Pseudocolochirus axiologus*
WATERS AROUND AUSTRALIA

SPIDERS – ARACHNIDA

Sydney Funnel-web   *Atrax rubustus*
NEW SOUTH WALES

Huntsman species *Holconia montana*
SOUTHERN AUSTRALIA

St Andrew's Cross Spider *Argiope keyserlingi*
EASTERN AUSTRALIA

Tasmanian Peacock Spider *Maratus tasmanicus*
SOUTH-EAST AUSTRALIA

Sapphire Rockmaster   *Diphlebia coerulescens*

Graphic Flutterer *Rhyothemis graphiptera*

NORTHERN AUSTRALIA

Blue-spotted Hawker *Adversaeschna brevistyla*
NORTHERN AND EASTERN AUSTRALIA

Bush cockroach species *Ellipsidion* sp.
AUSTRALIA

Grasshopper species *Methiola picta*
AUSTRALIA

Hibiscus Harlequin Bug *Tectocoris diophthalmus*

Antlion species Myrmeleontidae
AUSTRALIA-WIDE

French's Longicorn   *Batocera frenchi*

QUEENSLAND

Botany Bay Weevil *Chrysolopus spectabilis*
SOUTH-EAST AUSTRALIA

Triangles *Trigonodes hyppasia*
NORTHERN AUSTRALIA

Cairns Birdwing *Ornithoptera euphorion*

QUEENSLAND

Australian Admiral *Vanessa itea*

Common Brown *Heteronympha merope*
SOUTHERN AUSTRALIA

Common Lineblue *Prosotas nora*

QUEENSLAND

Spitfire sawfly larvae Pyrgidae
AUSTRALIA-WIDE

Cuckoo wasp species Chrysididae
AUSTRALIA-WIDE

Paper wasp species Vespidae
AUSTRALIA-WIDE

Bull ant species Formicidae

AUSTRALIA-WIDE

Chequered Cuckoo Bee   *Thyreus caeruleopunctatus*
AUSTRALIA-WIDE

Queen of Sheba Orchid *Thelymitra speciosa*

SOUTH-WEST WESTERN AUSTRALIA

Reaching Spider Orchid *Caladenia arrecta*
SOUTH-WEST WESTERN AUSTRALIA

Woolly-sepaled Eremophila *Eremophila lachnocalyx*
WESTERN AUSTRALIA

Pigface species   *Carpobrotus* sp.

AUSTRALIAN COASTS

Waratah *Telopea speciosissima*
NEW SOUTH WALES

Needlebush   *Hakea sericea*

SOUTH-EAST AUSTRALIA

Sydney Golden Wattle *Acacia longifolia*
SOUTH-EAST AUSTRALIA

Queensland Bottle Tree   *Brachychiton rupestris*
QUEENSLAND

Sturt's Desert Rose *Gossypium sturtianum*

AUSTRALIAN INTERIOR

Common Firebush *Keraudrenia integrafolia*
AUSTRALIAN INTERIOR

Curtain Fig *Ficus virens* var. *sublanceolata*
NORTHERN AND EASTERN AUSTRALIA

Powderpuff Lillypilly　*Syzygium wilsonii*

Swamp Bloodwood *Corymbia ptychocarpa*
NORTH-WEST AUSTRALIA

Anemone Stinkhorn *Aseroe rubra*
EASTERN AUSTRALIA

Coral fungus species *Clavaria* sp.

Pixie's Parasol *Mycena interrupta*
EASTERN AUSTRALIA

Ghost Mushroom *Omphalotus nidiformis*
SOUTHERN AUSTRALIA

Rainbow Bracket *Trametes versicolor*

SOUTHERN AND EASTERN AUSTRALIA

A Tribute to the Reptiles and Amphibians of Australia and New Zealand
Australian Herpetological Society
ISBN 978 1 92554 659 0

Australian Wildlife On Your Doorstep
Stephanie Jackson
ISBN 978 1 92554 630 9

Butterflies of the World
Adrian Hoskins
ISBN 978 1 92151 733 4

A Complete Guide to Reptiles of Australia
Fifth Edition
Steve Wilson and Gerry Swan
ISBN 978 1 92554 602 6

Crocodiles of the World
Colin Stevenson
ISBN 978 1 92554 628 6

Field Companion to the Mammals of Australia
Steve van Dyck, Ian Gynther and Andrew Baker (Eds)
ISBN 978 1 87706 981 9

A Field Guide to Butterflies of Australia
Garry Sankowsky and Geoff Walker
ISBN 978 1 92151 773 0

A Field Guide to Insects in Australia
Fourth Edition
Paul Zborowski and Ross Storey
ISBN 978 1 92 9781925546071

A Field Guide to Reptiles of New South Wales
Third Edition
Gerry Swan, Ross Sadlier and Glenn Shea
ISBN 978 1 92554 608 8

A Field Guide to Reptiles of Queensland
Second Edition
Steve Wilson
ISBN 978 1 92151 748 8

Insects of the World
Paul Zborowski
ISBN 978 1 92554 609 5

Rainforests of Australia's East Coast
Peter Krisch
ISBN 978 1 92554 629 3

Reed Concise Guide to Snakes of Australia
Gerry Swan
ISBN 978 1 92151 789 1

The Slater Field Guide to Australian Birds
Second Edition
Peter Slater, Pat Slater and Raoul Slater
ISBN 978 1 87706 963 5

Tropical Marine Fishes of Australia
Rick Stuart-Smith, Graham Edgar, Andrew Green
and Ian Shaw
ISBN 978 1 92151 761 7

Tropical Marine Life of Australia
Graham Edgar
ISBN 978 1 92151 758 7

Wild Dives
Nick and Caroline Robertson-Brown
ISBN 978 1 92554 642 2

Wild Leadership
Erna Walraven
ISBN 978 1 92554 635 4

In the same series as this title:
World of Birds
ISBN 978 1 92554 652 1

World of Butterflies
ISBN 978 1 92554 661 3

World of Insects
ISBN 978 1 92554 651 4

World of Mammals
ISBN 978 1 92554 660 6

World of Reptiles
ISBN 978 1 92554 653 8

For details of these books
and hundreds of other
Natural History titles see
www.newhollandpublishers.com
and follow ReedNewHolland
on Facebook and Instagram

First published in 2022 by Reed New Holland Publishers
Sydney

Level 1, 178 Fox Valley Road, Wahroonga, NSW 2076, Australia

newhollandpublishers.com

A record of this book is held at the National Library of Australia.

ISBN 978 1 92554 662 0

Managing Director: Fiona Schultz
Publisher and Project Editor: Simon Papps
Designer: Andrew Davies
Production Director: Arlene Gippert
Printed in China

10 9 8 7 6 5 4 3 2 1

Keep up with Reed New Holland
and New Holland Publishers
 ReedNewHolland
 @NewHollandPublishers and @ReedNewHolland

Front cover: Sugar Glider *Petaurus berviceps.*
Back cover: New Holland Honeyeater *Phylidonyris novaehollandiae*,
on Grevillea.
Page 1: Eastern Grey Kangaroo *Macropus giganteus.*
Pages 2–3: Rainbow Lorikeet *Trichoglossus haemotodus.*
Pages 4–5: Ulysses Swallowtail *Papilio ulysses.*